The World *of* Numbers

Where Did Middle Land Come From?

MARION TZUI YANG

Dedication

To Numbers 1 through 9, to squares & circles,
Last but not least, to my one-year-old, Mingzhi.
He presence pressed me to continue on.

A long, long time ago, there was a country called Middle Land. Middle Land was unique because it was built on nine numbers. Middle Land had no zero nor negative numbers. Midlanders used only one,

two, three, four, five, six, seven, eight, and nine. With these numbers, Midlanders created Suanpan, discovered Luoshu, established Shu-fa, designed Taichi, and even invented Go and Tangram.

How did Midlanders create their abacus, Suanpan? First, they invented a ruler of nine numbers, Ju. Then, they folded Ju in half. That made number 5 the head, and numbers 6, 7, 8, 9 and 4, 3, 2, 1 formed a pair of columns below it. After that, they doubled Ju.

1	2	3	4	5	6	7	8	9

For the framework of Suanpan, Midlanders applied the halved Ju for width and the doubled Ju for length. Then, they divided the frame in two: a much shorter upper section and a long lower one. They placed five counting beads one each of the 17 rods in the frame: one on top representing the head 5 and four below representing the paired columns: 1, 2, 3, 4 and 6, 7, 8, 9. To use it, start from the very right, and move the beads up and down the rod to count from 1 to 9. At 10, clear the rod and move one bead up on the rod to its left, and so on. Today, people around the world are still using this ancient calculator.

1 2 3 4 5 6 7 8 9 9 8 7 6 5 4 3 2 1

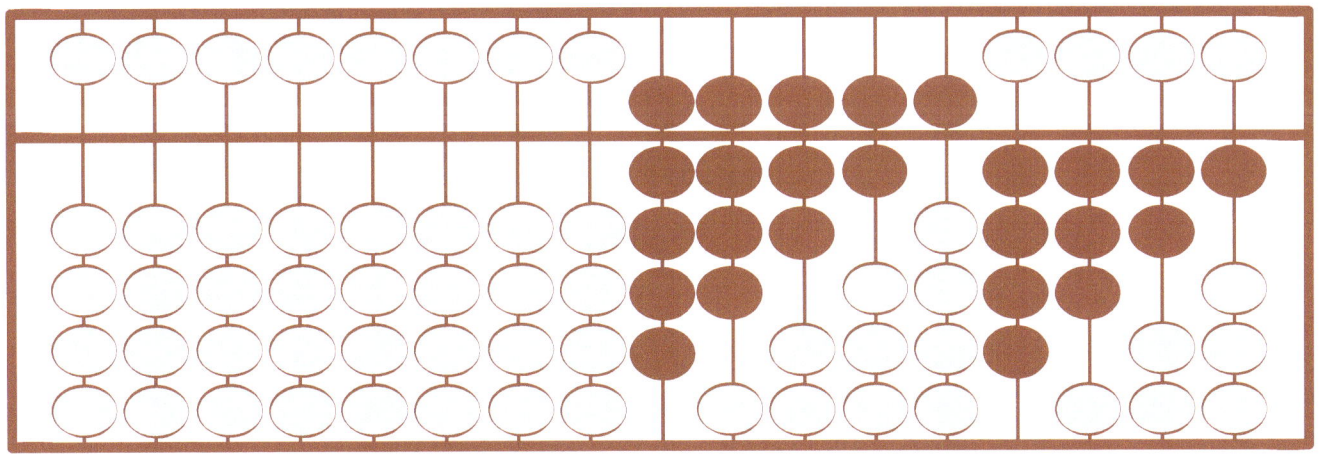

9 8 7 6 5 4 3 2 1

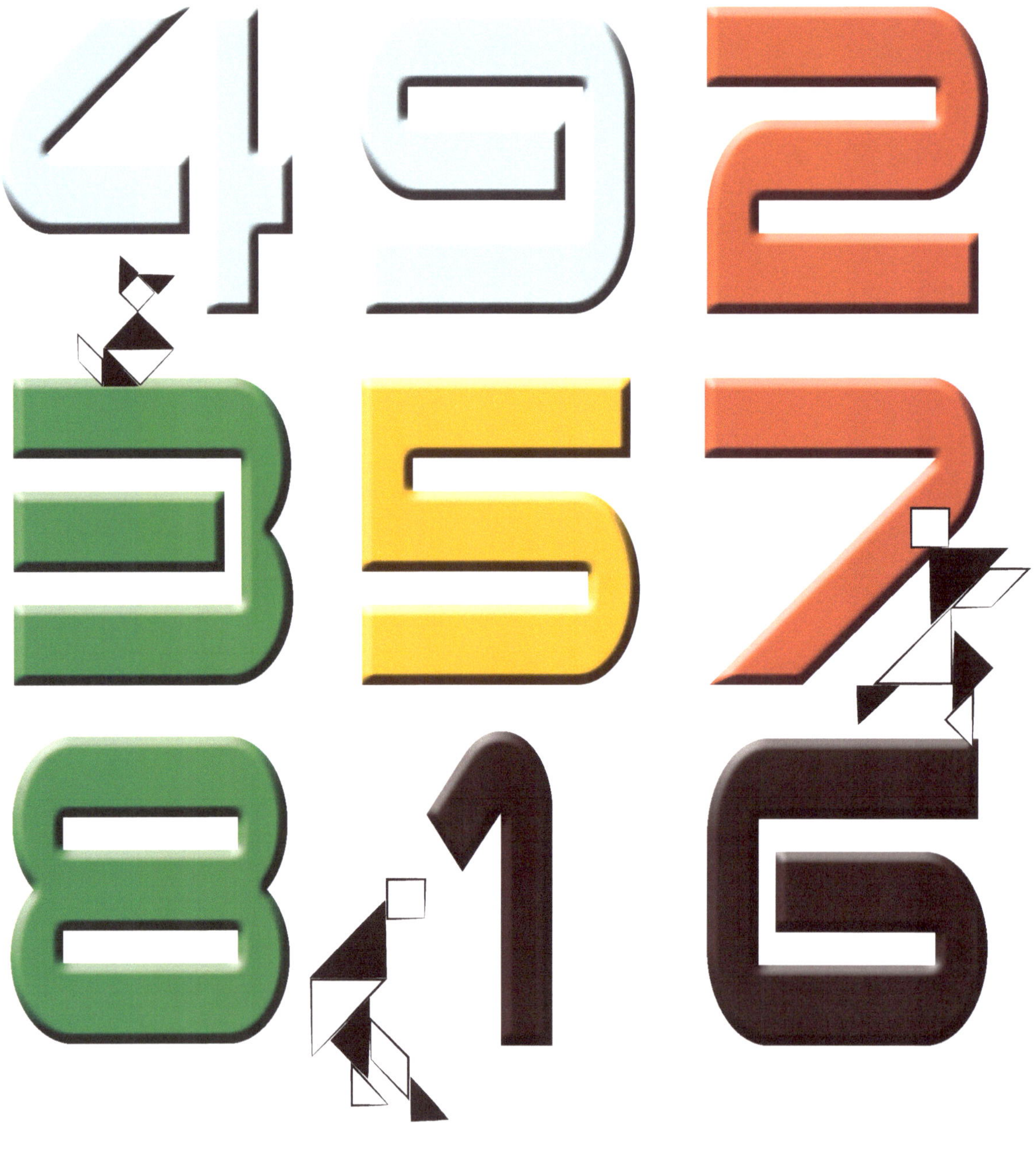
4 9 2
3 5 7
8 1 6

From the ruler Ju, Midlanders learned that all symmetrically paired numbers looking on either side of the middle 5 have the same sum of 10. That is,

$$1+9 = 2+8 = 3+7 = 4+6$$

From the abacus Suanpan, Midlanders further learned that numbers from paired column which the same counting bead represents in its lower section have the same difference of 5. That is,

$$6-1 = 7-2 = 8-3 = 9-4$$

Once more Midlanders placed number 5 in the center, and they strung the remaining eight numbers to surround it, forming the word rice, 米. These numbers looked across at each other like those on the ruler Ju, and they paired up like those in the lower section of the abacus Suanpan. As a result, the sum total of each row, column, and diagonal line all adds up to 15. For such a discovery, Midlanders wrote a book, *Luoshu*. Contemporary mathematics categorizes it as Magic Square.

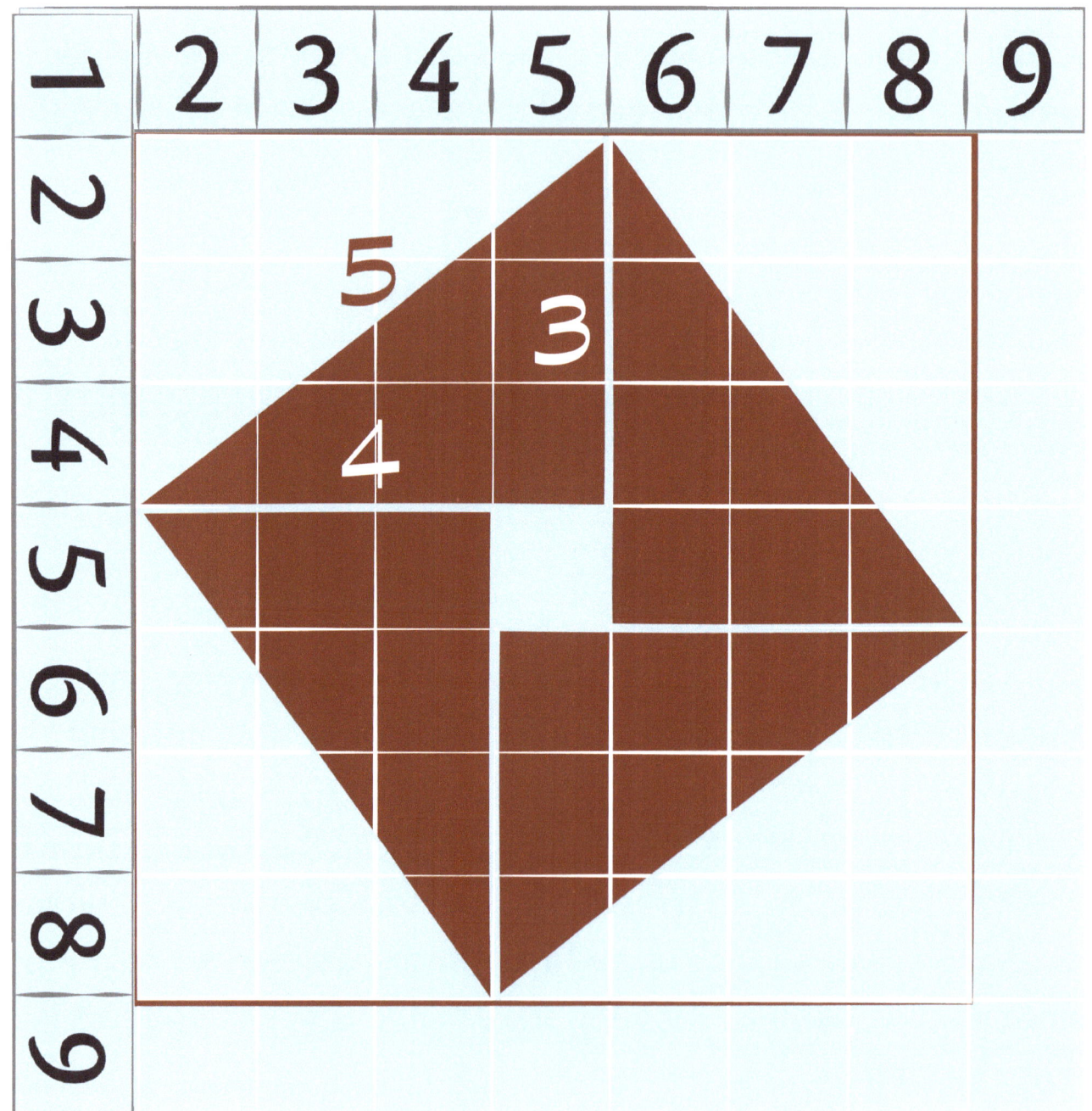

For Midlanders, however, the real magic square is the square of Ju, 9x9=81. From this square they established their laws in mathematics, Shufa.

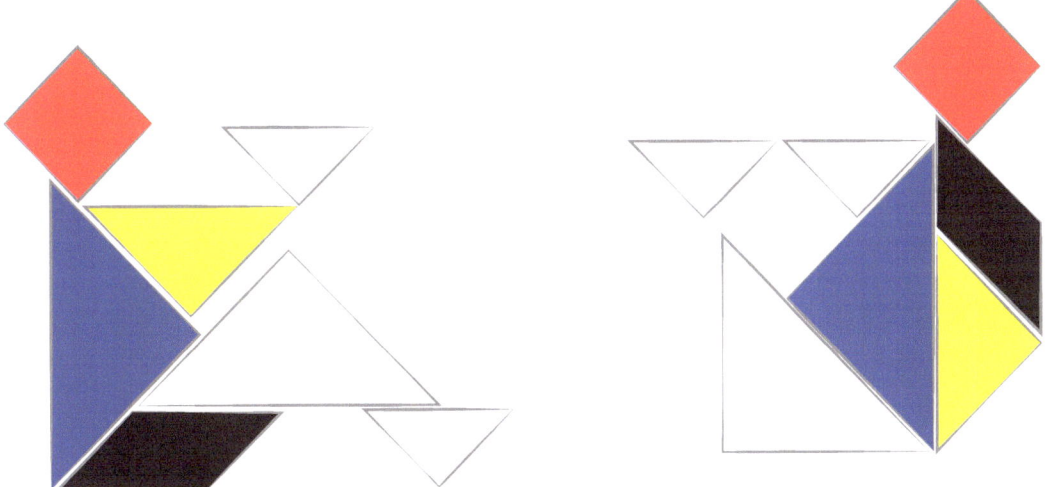

To start, Midlanders dissected both rulers on either side of the square in the center and found out that a square is composed of four right triangles and the center. All of the triangles have identical sides of 3 and 4 and 5. This was an important discovery, upon which Midlanders could measure the distance between any given objects. Today, they call this a theorem by Shanggao. Contemporary mathematics calls it the Pythagorean theorem.

Shanggao said, "Shufa comes from [dissecting] circles and squares. Circles come from [dissecting] squares." Now that they had the perfect square of 5x5, Midlanders continued, they wondered what the perfect circle would be.

Since a square is composed of four right triangles and a center, the circle that comes from it should also have a center and four circular shapes in equal footing.

Midlanders started by simplifying the square by coloring it in yin (black) and yang (white). Then, they made another square inside it, and another, and another. Each time a square was made, the center got smaller. While all squares were moving in a circular formation, their center remained the same.

Around this center, four circular shapes emerged from designing a circle. By using a fuzzy set and its five subsets to present this perfect circle, we can pin down its five true values: More Yang, Less Yang, Middle (or Center), Less Yin, and More Yin.

More Yang

Less Yang

Middle

Less Yin

More Yin

These values in contemporary math are five subsets of a fuzzy system. However, in faraway Middle Land and from a long time ago, Midlanders assigned five elements in Nature to them. Throughout their history, Midlanders have created multiple applications of the very same system in all walks of life.

In short, they assigned "Fire" to More Yang, and "Wood" to Less Yang. They assigned "Metal" to Less Yin, "Water" to More Yin, and "Land" to the center of the circle, Middle.

These five true values have since become an important attribution to their language as well. For example, when Midlanders built their country, they called its central government, Middle Land. Today, more so than before, they are calling both their country and their language Middle.

Now that Midlanders had the perfect circle from the perfect square, they made it the eternal symbol of a fuzzy system, and called it Tai-chi. This is partly because it takes the forms of Tai-yin and Tai-yang swirling seamlessly together to represent More Yin and More Yang, and partly because it illuminates an ultimate (chi) deduction in mathematics of infinity with Less Yin and Less Yang emerging from More Yang and More Yin.

Simply put, Wood, Fire, Earth, Metal, and Water are both the Nature and the writing on the wall in Middle Land. It was especially noticeable in areas of martial arts and medicine because Midlanders have by and large defined their physical world according to these five values.

Not only in the martial arts and medicine, but also in the literature, a reservoir of Human-Nature expressions were thus created. For example, all colors an eye could see were "five colors," all sounds an ear could hear were "five notes," and all tastes a tongue could tell were "five flavors." They also assigned colors to these values. And because Metal (white) comes before Water (black) by the natural order, "black and white" has since had an implied meaning of upside down.

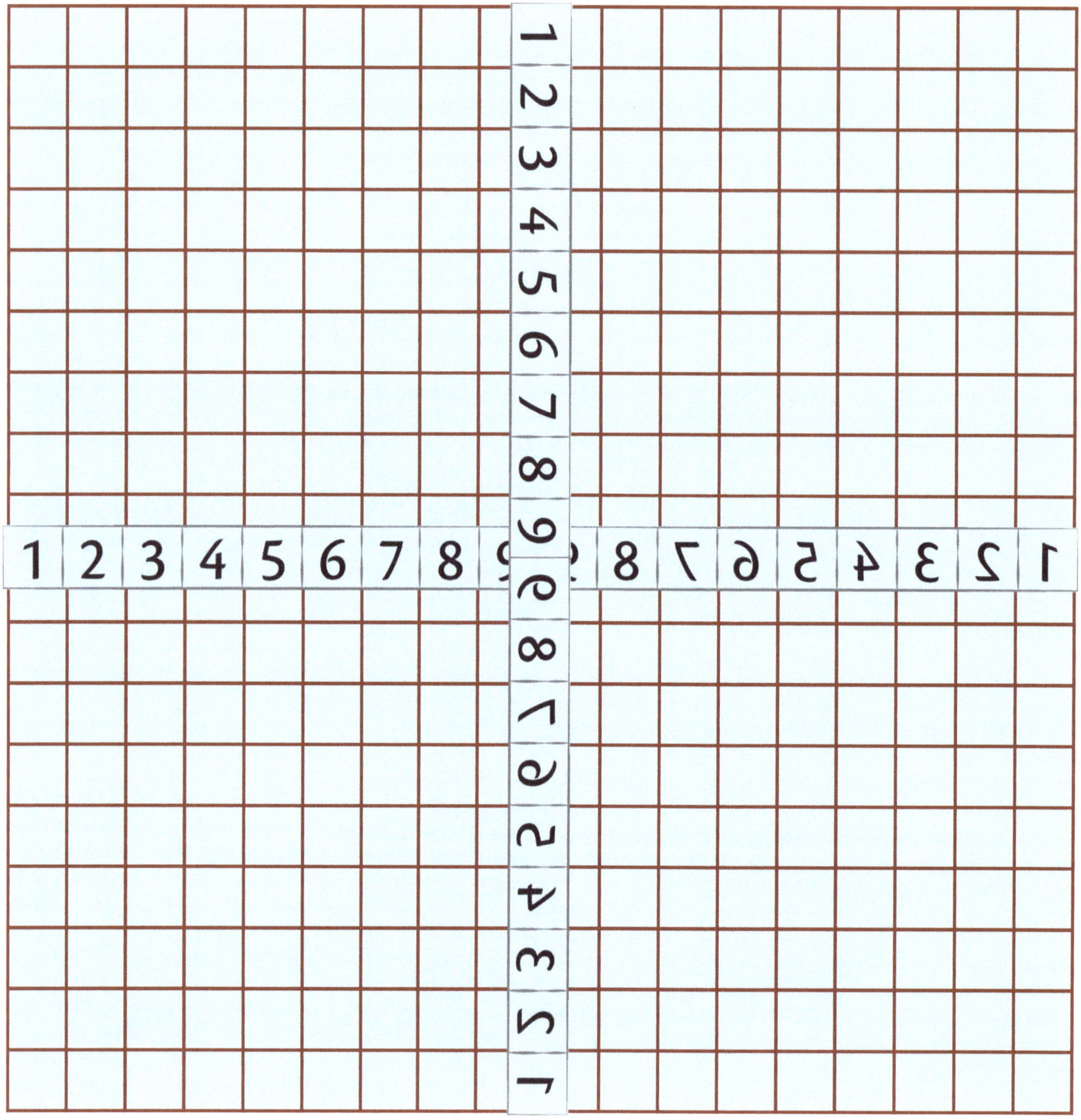
1 2 3 4 5 6 7 8 9

The infinity of math can also be found in the game of Go.

To make a Go board, Ju was doubled and then squared. This 18x18 square was marked by 19x19 grids, 361 intersecting points. The grids represent a network of lifeline for Go pieces, 360 of them. Go pieces are round, half of them are painted in black, the other half white, to represent two players for the game.

Go is about occupation and survival. It has three rules. One, occupy. Take turn to place as many Go pieces at any available points as possible. Two, attack. Take the opponent's piece(s) prisoner by occupying (blocking) all immediate neighboring points of its/their occupancy. Three, counter attack. Strategize to keep getting points without getting the lifeline cut off at the same time. At the end of the game, whoever accumulates more points wins.

Today, not one application can compute all the movements a Go player may or may not make in the game yet. The strategies of Go are infinitely many.

The invention of Tangram has nothing to do with the invention of Ju, but with its many applications in the world of numbers. Although simple, the varied and many design people have done with Tangram proves the game is as infinitely intricate as that of Go.

The making of Tangram starts with halving a square (red) into two right triangles (white). Then, two variations of regrouping these triangles form another right triangle (yellow) and a rectangle (black). Doubling the yellow triangle by combining the red square and yellow triangle gives the largest triangle (blue) in the diagram. As a result, Tangram consists of seven tans in five different shapes (shown in five different colors here).

To play the Tangram puzzle is to design abstract pieces. A player's imagination is the only limitation. Since it was invented, hundreds of thousands of shapes have been designed and recorded. Today, players can start by playing with them to enjoy the challenges of geometry and the fun of abstract!

This is more or less how Midlanders halved, doubled, squared, and circled round and round a simple ruler of Ju to create Suanpan, discover and write *Luoshu*, establish Shufa, design Taichi, and invent Go and Tangram!

In the summer of 2012, I designed my own Sudoku game. I applied my imaginary ruler Ju to a square cradled hardboard. Then I populated the board with 81 wood blocks. I designed 9 blocks and made 9 sets of them. Each block has on it a number on 2 opposite sides, a color that matches each number on another 2 opposite sides, and two black and white circle versus square patterns on the remaining 2 sides. With these blocks, I can play Sudoku not only in numbers but also in colors and in mixed numbers and colors. I can even play mini Go with the black and white patterns.

This homemade fuzzy Sudoku became the precedent of my second game, Taichi Cube. Simply put, I redesigned the 3x3 Magic Cube from the 1970's by rendering all six sides of the nine blocks from my Sudoku onto the cube. This cube incorporated fuzzy logic and magic square. It also took me back to the distant Middle Land.

In Middle Land I saw an abacus, a magic square, the perfect square and its perfect circle. I saw a game of life and a diagram of imagination. Last but not least, I saw a simple ruler and an infinite world.

www.ingramcontent.com/pod-product-compliance
Lightning Source LLC
Chambersburg PA
CBHW041830280526
45792CB00006B/2041